THE BLUE TORTOISE

HAIKU POEMS

BERNARD FILIPOW

The Blue Tortoise
Copyright © 2021 by Bernard Filipow

Tellwell Talent
www.tellwell.ca

ISBN
978-0-2288-4974-2 (Hardcover)
978-0-2288-4972-8 (Paperback)
978-0-2288-4973-5 (eBook)

Books by Bernard Filipow

AMORESIA: Love Sonnets

To my granddaughter, Peyton Taylor Filipow, and my grandsons, Marcus Filipow, Everest and Ethan Mandy.

In Japanese culture, the tortoise is the symbol for wisdom, luck, protection and longevity. Its shell and underside are also believed to unite heaven and earth.

THE BLUE TORTOISE
HAIKU POEMS

THE POEMS

Precious memories
Sculpted in white oak go 'round
My mind's carousel

My heart is a bird
In a gilded cage singing
Of migrating winds

When the rains pour down
My eyes see only rainbows
Dreams of thunder clouds

In the early morn
The play of light and shadows
Excite our gardens

Your heart is a diamond
Set in a platinum ring
Of my devotion

Starlings in the sky
Murmurate in fly patterns
Neighbours to seven

A butterfly kiss
Dries tears and comforts children
Honours the milk weed

Paradigm of love
Sweet and ever unfolding
Thief of summer's light

Strong winds off the lake
The willow waved as they passed
Oaks snapped in half

The lightening flashed
I listened for the thunder
It is a given

At night in the cold
The candle flickers and fades
A beacon of hope

A cold winter's night
Soft snowflakes tickling my face
Walking Summer Street

Walking in the dark
Looking for a shooting star
Trying to decide

No one has seen it
It's passport is its cargo
Birds, butterflies and…

The icicles drip
The south wind blows warm and soft
I hear the robin

A frightened horse runs
It's an animal of flight
A constellation

Love travels like wind
With no need of a passport
Just an open heart

Leaves curl like a flute
And the cool north wind breaths out
An ode "tooo" winter

The "princess tree" grows
And surfs waves of seven seas
With a fate that's sealed

The deer broke its leg
And wolves ate the injured deer
"She" can be cruel

There was a pink moon
The year's largest supermoon
Spring flowers rejoiced

Tuna pods circled
Schools of herring in the bay
Like fishermen's nets

Blossoms drop to ground
Who knows if fruit trees will bear?
Spring sprang too early

Charms' hums evanesce
Emeralds and cochineals
Kissing blossoms deep

The squirrel escaped
The claws of the red-tailed hawk
But not the cart's wheel

Flakes of corn snow fall
The daffodils bow their heads
We're in equinox

The writer sowed verses
While snow fell on his garden
In spring, poets bud

Floating on zephyrs
The kite spirals on its way
To construct a bridge

Our garden thaws
Spring brings a resurrection
Winter is pardoned

Acromatia
Replaced with fauvist splendour
Aureus returns

Spring winds prune the trees
Blossoms kissed by honey bees
Promises to keep

Geese migrate above
In darkness guided by stars
As blind raptors sleep

The cardinal sings
In the slow fading twilight
Messages in bottled

Up before daylight
The birds sing the dawn chorus
To the rising sun

Deep in northern woods
Armed snowflakes whisper secrets
In ancient starlight

Diving shadows "cawed"
And young robins "cherilied"
How silent the spring

Out of the southwest
They migrate with a tailwind
Guided by the stars

The heron landed
In a secret garden pond
Of living jewels

On a sea of green
I rode waves of daffodils
To the end of spring

At the equinox
Sun paths due east to due west
Circling the globe

Blossoms tilt their heads
Routing hummers kiss them deep
En route from Tunis

Solemn is the spring
As apricot blossoms fall
To bees' sacred hum

Waves gleam in the night
As dolphins and surfers sparkle
"Soakin' up the glow"

Skies paint the waters
With the colours of weather
Guided by the wind

The salmon was caught
And covered with many stones
Circling were eagles

The branch is a hawk
And the squirrel climbs the tree
Inevitable?

"Tooth of the lion"
Herba non receperint
But don't piss the bed!

Old Onguiaahra
A gulp of cormorants dives
In your water's flow

So lost and alone
No sisters to guide my way
I tighten my belt

Their hum is sacred
So like the human spirit
Reveal bee prophets

In the leaves a face
Recognized from long ago
Now gone in the wind

Stomach, chest and head
The power of breathing life
"Momento mori!"

Eagles survey pools
Salmon swim deeper by day
Upstreaming by night

Apple or cherry
With aromas and warmth
Sailing to Delos

Sacred to the gods
Whose heads were crowned with their
leaves
Which hid the Green Man

The doe tried luring
They were working an odor
And they found the fawn

His beloved passed
With grief inconsolable
Wrote sonnets sublime

Gusts blew through the trees
Windfalls scattered on the ground
Geese fed and sought shade

The snows came early
Covering verdant landscape
In melting tlapi

The wind blew ice cold
Snow ghosts danced across the field
Chased by a lost hound

Precious memories
Fill one with profound yearning
So sweet, so cruel

When I speak of them
I am lost for words and weep
They are my children!

I assessed the tree
Pruning offending branches
As if a court judge

Black flies aplenty
Surgeons of the Margaree
Salmon were running

When in the Rockies
I thought I heard kettle drums
Sounding like thunder

The concerto fades
"Pianississississimo"
I have ascended

The sun surrenders
Colours fade into darkness
I am now at peace

Sacred to this god
Who wore a crown of their leaves
And "splashed" in the rain

The eagle landed
On the shore of the river
Salmon flashed silver

The adagio
So tranquil and exquisite
Introduced Stendhal

Unfinished splendour
With eighteen towers to build
To glorify one

In a southwest wind
Blossoms fall like tears of bees
To songs of migrants

Old man holds child's hand
Winter and spring together
As in one season

I dismounted
'Twas the eye of the eagle
That looked back at me

There is a sadness
Blossoms fall in wind and rain
But hope fruit will set

In the early spring
Dapples of morning sunlight
Speckle my garden

Treasured memories
Root deep like oaks in my mind
Sacred to my soul

In the heat of day
The road shimmered before me
I heard a rooster crow

I cast the spinner
A backlash returned the lure
And hooked my young hand

I have never known why
I dislike sparrows so much
So unlike the hawk

On a sunny day
My shadow is the colour
Of the blue heron

She lost all her teeth
What one saw was her soul and
Beauty of being

I asked "Who am I?"
Then once again "Who am I?"
Again "Who am I?"

In the heat of day
I move slow and carefully
Like the blue tortoise

In indifference
It seemed I had found freedom
Like a bird in flight

Of all spring flowers
She was the most beautiful
Our soil had produced

My aging body
Is but a tabernacle
For my timeless soul

He found a dead coon
And cut off some of its hair
To tie caddis flies

The landmark oak fell
Its dying thunderclap lost
In the wild spring wind

Thoughts of you persist
But I know not where you are
Except in my dreams

The sea wind breathless
Tide over in the grey dawn
Waiting butterflies

At the piano
Pencil from mouth to soundboard
Inspired by moonlight

La Seine at Chatou
Skiffs with dames in summer's light
Colours so intense

So old and fragile
Her eyes sparkling fire diamonds
Her soul a phoenix

O Mount Fuji-San
You sleep with one eye open
When will you wake up?

"Protector of Man"
You solved the puzzle of knots
And conquered Asia

It only comes once
The love that outlives starlight
Once in a lifetime

Its peak has been reached
My garden is full and lush
Rain was plentiful

It struck the window
A blood heart appeared on stone
Then it flew away

The road is icy
And I walk like an old dog
On a frozen pond

Two boys watering
A fountain filled with pansies
Croise in the wind

O Mount Fuji-San
Your temperature is rising
Why are you incensed?

Orange clouds behind trees
With changing faces of leaves
Slow-fade to twilight

Skating on pink ponds
Joined by meandering streams
Not feeling my feet

In the April rain
I danced around the puddles
As if on a cloud

He rode his bike far
Just to see them galloping
Across the meadow

As candles flickered
Memories danced in my mind
Some spring, some winter

So ingenious
The squirrels at the feeder
So like acrobats

Is that a bluejay
Or is it a mockingbird
Imitating one?

I hear the gunshots
Duck hunters on the river
The sun at their backs

A stand of cedars
After a mid-winter storm
Were candles on cake

I looked at the tree
And saw a face in the leaves
It could have been mine

After the downpour
There was the gentlest breeze
An apology

Alstroemeria
"Majestic Henri" in bloom
Passed unnoticed

The nighthawk peent calls
I sit in the potting shed
Connected to all

The beagle got lost
Following the rabbits scent
Now it was hunted

In the quiet woods
Deep realities open
I am enlightened

My horse's nostrils flare
He dislikes the smell of pigs
Unlike the Romans

How will I survive
Without the spring in her smile
Autumn on her cheek?

In the afterglow
Old loves faded in the past
Reignite in stars

Lying in the hay
I wondered of my purpose
Is it to evolve?

When he is frightened
My horse becomes Pegasus
A constellation

The scent of a rose
Excites my olfactory sense
To its perfection

A rainbow pheasant
Glided in front of my horse
And I too took flight

My secret prayer
Is to die in my garden
There closest to God

In the horse stable
There were many lessons learned
But who remembered?

My old skates hang still
After many years on ice
And dreams in my youth

One cannot forget
The sight of eagles in flight
For it is regal

The oak split in two
Like the parting between we two
Damn the devil wind!

My dog wandered far
After many days searching
She was "in the wind"

They stood like driftwood
As they cast flies from the shore
To where salmon lie

I released the scrod
To a fierce golden fury
Of wings, beak and claws

With her worn knees bent
An old women crossed the pond
Singing beneath her

No one knows just when
Here one day and gone the next
The circus has flown

If I think of you
Are you thinking of me too?
Why am I sneezing?

In the summer heat
The salmon lie deep in shallow pools
And run in the night

Why climb a mountain?
The great Mallory said,
"Because it is there!"

Rome swoops high above
As joyous as a skylark
Her spirit devine

Care for my children
And know I will care for yours
For they are all "ours"!

Four sides of a barn
With links to Mars and Saturn
A feast and a foe

Climbing mountains
One does not know what prevails
And if storms await

Down the Horseshoe Falls
Flows the great Niagara
Swift to meet the sky

Succulent peaches
From Niagara orchards
Should be eaten wild

Sun dance and soft seas
Sails slant on the horizon
Could be anywhere

The summer sun dove
Into scenic Lake Huron
Splashing fire skyward

When day fades to night
Its beauty and mystery
Beg the question "Why?"

When night breaks for day
Its new beginnings and dreams
Fill us with "Hope!"

Protecting its young
The robin swooped over head
I praised its bravery

Pink cherry blossoms
In a sad drizzle of spring
Parachute to ground

Light fades to dark
Snuffed out by the horizon
The afterglow beams

In the stifling heat
The voice of a cicada
Was heard from somewhere

Bitten by bed bugs
The sheets were covered in blood
Building the railway

In misty meadows
Dreams become reality
In songs of the lark

I sat listening
To the rhythm of my breath
Like a clock ticking

What to plant and where
A gardener's dilemma
Like water and rain

Nasal honks of geese
Pass overhead in the night
Guided by instincts

Smiling but frowning
Suspicious distorted faces
How I distrust clowns

I did dream of it
"Pure joy free of sadness"
But never lived it!

The church bells chimed
To celebrate the event
As rain fell like rice

The bride looked lovely
Her Italian family cried
The groom smoked a cigar

The noisy snow geese
Migrating high overhead
Were lost and then found

When they descended
They appeared like a snow globe
Of nasal honking

Parched leaves weep tears
In rays of golden sunlight
After autumn rains

Siroccos took her hat
Cars in all directions stopped
She was "Athena"

Lunar chariot
Driven across the heavens
To light the night sky

Night and day and night…
Winking eyes open and close
The full moon rises

Descending mountains
Though harder then climbing them
Is where beauty lies

Grass was green and soft
As we carried him to bury
Robins sang "cheer-up"

From shallow cliff scrapes
Wanderers stooping for prey
Like skyworld spirits

The sun dove to sea
And was lost beneath its waves
Splashing fire to sky

A bird lost in leaves
Sings its song to a nest mate
There is no answer

A flash of silver
Suddenly breaks the surface
"O salmo salar!"

Fluky winds and rain
The horn blows the race is won
The chill lasts for hours

Like the pious farmer
I harvest the colours of fall
To feed winter verse

Favourite season?
I'm a man for all seasons!
Especially spring!

I lie awake nights
Thinking of indiscretions
To forgive/forget

One can sense the change
As leaves chafe in the sad wind
To birds' autumn song

After all these years
Alone in quiet darkness
I still dance with you

Orchid seeds now set
Scythers mow the meadowlands
Midst shafts of sunlight

Elysium bound
Kiting on a spider's web
Destiny prevails

Sacred memories
That paralyze my being
Still weep in my dreams

In the cool morning
I hear the robin's autumn song
To summer's passing

Lemon tree blossoms
Welcome hummers in the morn
And in winter dreams

I heard the owl call
In the middle of the night
"Who cooks for you all?"

In his brother's arms
Between colours of twilight
A death to be wished?

Thieves of day's sunlight
Sweet scented growths unfolding
Messengers of love

Blinking wanderer
Waiting on migrating winds
With no lips to kiss

Princes of Orange
Shower my gardens in gold
Blossoms' sovereigns

Blue birds fly away
Swaying in the morning breeze
An empty feeder

Thawing icicles
Drip on daffodils below
To a robin's song

Drizzle calms the night
As frogs in my garden "croke"
Their love serenade

A bevy of doves
Spirit messengers to all
Bring much inner peace

I lie on the grass
At once I feel connected
"Canadiana"

The northwest wind blows
As hummers dance on pine boughs
Is it time to leave?

My horse, Aureus,
Weighs eleven hundred pounds
Shies at windswept leaves

Autumn snowflakes fall
They are as light as pappi
Its nature's segway

Monarchs square to wind
Sit steady on the pine boughs
Waiting luftpauses

"Where did we come from?"
And "To where are we going?"
Life's big mysteries

The pub was crowded
The old man sat "loon lonely"-
Not to be disturbed!

Moored in the river
An island unto myself
I ask and answer

Cool fall rain fell straight
On fading roses and pines
With no birds in sight

The fall rains pulsed
Like an arhythmic heart beat
Fluttering then slow

Dawn exhales the night
Flights of dreams inconsequence
Breath words into verse

As maple leaves fall
Day gives way to early night
Thief of the days light

Henna body art
Tattoos up and down their arms
Thank you Captain Cook!

The siren was lost
In southern Sirocco winds
Quadri did not close

Such brotherly love
Two sunflowers in a vase
In Auvers sur Oise

Autumn fruitfulness
Harvest festivals and mists
Impenetrable

Black flies a plenty...
Am I tourist or Canuck?
I will not complain!

My crowned fedora
"Puni soit qui mal y pense"
Reigns atop my head

As their colours age
And leaves fall in autumn winds
Landscapes are reborn

Crying without tears
On a day we knew would come
For a bud to bloom

Two garden statues
Masquerading as mute swans
With roses plier

Sitting in the park
The old man flipped komboloi
His thoughts years away

The autumn twilight
With melancholy colours
Welcomes early night

Trapped in the currents
Swans were swept over the falls
To talus below

"Peaked like an arrow
And it could split a raindrop!"
The old farmer's roof

I lie awake nights
Visited by the black dog
And great ideas

As I lay dying
Of what will be my last thoughts?
I can't imagine!

Peyton slipped and fell
"Were you wearing your slippers?"
"Come again Nono!"

"Princes of orange"
Leaves fell on sawtoothed pumpkins
Awaiting the night

Icebergs in currents
Navigate in crystal dawn
To the horizon

Circling in whirlpools
The hunters in camouflage
Rescued injured swans

Indian Summer
Thoughts of youthful happiness
Tis the time to hunt!

Fall dressed in colour
Fades to acromatia
In the cold north wind

I thought there was more
But I was terribly wrong
And lost what I had

Sweetgums bore their souls
As rich colours of autumn
Revealed their secrets

On the Lake at night
Floating beneath the starry sky
Sensing life beyond

"Mad, bad ... dangerous!"
Loved as hero and poet
Greek's immortal child

The pale horse was wild
And ran with our precious breath
With no cure in sight

Sculpted by the rains
Painted by colours of sky
Flows a masterpiece

Aquila flies high
Paying homage to Eos
As heavens open

The slush was heavy
Snapping sycamore branches
Crackled in the night

A horse in the pines
Piaffes in the winter wind
Midst dustings of snow

Hanging from a tree
By catgut around its neck
Its only crime, flight

In the eastern sky
Shades of hope colour the dawn
To an enigma

In her chariot
Neither a star nor a planet
Cynthia protects us

Animal instincts
And risks taken finding mates
Who can explain it?

Brandishing a scythe
A rider on a pale horse
Stole our breath away

Pests at bird-feeders
Uninvited visitors
The bragging should stop

The soldiers stood in a line
Like a hedge of emeralds
I could smell the cedar

The early snows fell
Turning the landscape to a
"Tabula rasa"!

A fly on the wall
I am tempted to swat it
But, open the window

Snows on the tundra
Acromatic playground
"Ooopacarophiles!"

Stable doors open
Horses frolic in the snow
Like children at play

The snow falling swirled
Cedars bowed in reverence
A saviour was born

At the quarter pole
The race is over for many
Beginning for some

Purging the rainbow
Gives way to red and orange
The fire stirs my soul

Niqirtsuitug lights
The Arctic treeless and pure
With sunsets sublime

I'm sure it was you
On the wings of a sweet dream
I wanted to stay